photo by
Francesco Barasciutti

# SOTTSASS
## Glass Works

*Edited by*
**Marino Barovier**
**Bruno Bischofberger**
**Milco Carboni**

**ARNOLDSCHE**

*Photography*
The publisher would like to thank the following
for their kind permission to reproduce the photographs:

Aldo Ballo
14/15
Francesco Barasciutti
13, 16, 17, 19, 20, 21, 23, 25, 26, 27, 29, 30, 31, 71, 108, 109, 110, 111,
112/113, 114, 115, 118, 119, 121, 122, 123, 125, 127, 129, 131, 133,
135, 137, 139, 140, 141, 142, 143, 144, 145, 146
Santi Caleca
33, 34, 35, 36, 37, 39, 40, 41, 42, 43, 45, 46, 47, 50, 51, 55, 56, 57, 59,
60, 61, 63, 67, 68, 69, 103, 104, 105, 106
Erick Hesmerg
92, 93, 95, 97, 98, 99, 101
Studio Pointer
75, 79, 80, 81, 83, 85, 87, 89, 90, 91

*Acknowledgments*
The publisher would like to thank the following for their precious help:

Alberto Albricci, Liana Cavallaro, Amelio Cenedese, Antonio Da Ros, Paolo Da Ros, Antonella Provasi, Giovanna Solinas, Gigi Toso, Luciano Vistosi

and

Marina Barovier Gallery, Venice
Galerie Bruno Bischofberger, Zürich

*Published by*
Arnoldsche Verlagsanstalt GmbH, Senefelder Straße 8
D–70178 Stuttgart

*Reproduced by*
Fotolito Veneta, Verona

*Printed in Italy by*
Rumor, Vicenza

*Die Deutsche Bibliothek – CIP-Einheitsaufnahme*
**Sottsass, Ettore**
Glass works / Sottsass. Ed. by Marino Barovier; Bruno Bischofberger; Milco Carboni
Stuttgart: Arnoldsche, 1998



**ISBN 3-925369-79-1**

# Contents

# Glass

## by Ettore Sottsass

I

When you design glass objects and even hope to make them, or hope someone will make them for you, you go through roughly three exciting moments.
The first is when you think you've got an idea and think – or flatter yourself – that the idea really is an idea, that it really is a strange apparition, somehow emerging from the general confusion of ideas which actually boils down to nothing, to the nothingness that was and suddenly is no more – because the idea has occurred; a nothingness – as has often been said – that has suddenly been enlightened.

The second is when you see that the glass, or its design, is about to be turned into glass. You know it is going to become glass, but you can't yet make it out. You see a sort of ghost of what the glass will be, a limp, shining and colourless ghost, red-hot, untouchable and elusive, as most ghosts are – they say – like flames, fire and the light of fire.

I have never actually made glass with my own hands, I have never blown into the long blowing iron to make a piece of glass, and I don't think I would even be capable of picking a gob of burning glass out of the lake of red-hot glass at the bottom of the "*boca del forno*" ... I know absolutely nothing about these risks and pleasures, and I certainly never will know anything about these secret pockets of knowledge. It only remains for me to stand and watch the people who do possess that knowledge.
The second especially exciting moment comes precisely when you go into one of those enormous rooms with their white, warm and silent air; warm on account of all the heat that comes out of the furnaces where the glass is soft; and silent because the men who work in those large white rooms wear tennis shoes or maybe special slippers, and talk in low voices. Perhaps they don't even speak at all, because each man knows so clearly what he has to do that there is no need to talk ...
In those big rooms, small clusters of silent men move around the bright and colourless

glass as it begins to take shape. As in the ballet of a magic rite, the men come and go, squashing and stretching the glass, inflating and cutting it, carrying lumps of it and slicing bits off it, drawing threads and attaching other morsels, twisting tubes and bringing in wood, throwing water and performing an enormous number of unwavering, miraculous gestures and all the time holding the glass in mid-air while it slowly acquires form ... those men in tennis shoes, those men who make no noise, have to keep the glass forever in mid-air, because the soft glass would always like to drop onto the ground, maybe because glass originates from the earth, from sand and dust ...

When I go into those big white very hot rooms, with the shadows of fires dancing on the walls, and the men's eyes folded onto the idea that a piece of glass must be made, that the glass has to be transformed into an object, that the glass will have a colour, a measure and a weight, that it will have a sense; that it will pass from one hand to another, from one space to the next, I gape; and if that glass on which all those men are concentrating their bent, attentive, lost gaze, is a piece of glass that perhaps came into my own head, then the surprise takes my breath away, I stand there open-mouthed like an idiot and ask myself: "What's happening?" "How is this possible?"

To tell the truth, I don't quite know how a thought which came to my mind about a glass and only existed as a thought, can sometimes become a drawing, which is only there as a drawing. But then the drawing becomes glass and the glass is there only as glass, a glass object that can be touched, weighed and broken, or put away you can't remember where – perhaps it's been stolen – but no, it's turned up again ...

The passage from the drawing to the glass that exists only as glass, always seems a miraculous one. So miraculous that I don't really know where I come into the picture at all, since I'm not somebody who works miracles. Then I remember the men in tennis shoes, the clustered silent men who possess the wisdom, who know the rules and the boundaries, the secret tensions and hardness and timing, who know all the temperatures and weights and everything there is to be known about how to look at a drawing and turn it into glass ...

If they weren't there, would my glass objects be there? Would they be the way they are? ...

The third moment is, of course, the triumphant one.

Not always. There are times when the glass comes out of the muffle, from the cooling

tunnel, in broken bits. But nearly always the glistening molten glass has agreed to let itself be cooled and to show its real colour. All this however has to happen slowly, very slowly, very very slowly, for hours, maybe whole nights, maybe days on end ... you have to be patient.
In the end, though, the glass is there.
It comes out of the fire all clean, intact, bright and perfect, exactly as you thought it would and maybe even more. At last the glass is there and can even be touched ...

## II

When I designed my first glass objects (about twenty-five years ago), I had already done a lot of ceramics. They were done in Tuscany and I think those first glass pieces done for Luciano Vistosi were deeply affected by my earlier Tuscan experiences.
I was trying then to design very simple things. They certainly were not minimalist (an existential choice of no concern to me). I wanted to design things that would somehow get me back to the origins of language, to that very mysterious time when the curiosity of untamed man was certainly not at its "minimum" but rather at its "maximum". I'm talking about the period when untamed men were trying desperately, with signs and speech, to design an identity for themselves among the animals on the planet.
Twenty-five years ago (and perhaps even now) I was trying to rediscover a fragment of those deposits of dust from history, fragments of the sandstone rocks which can still be found here and there, in abandoned quarries, and are a record of the very slow stratification of the figure of human "essence".
I was not trying then to design some sort of absolute, some sort of representation of the divine, or any – long since lost – purity or any metaphysical perfection. I was trying – at least trying – to recapture a trace of that modicum of "archaic" curiosity or necessity (not of desire) that survives in our earthly destiny as men ...
Too ambitious? ...

## III

At the end of the Sixties and later during the Seventies, problems tended, generally speaking, to multiply, and also to get very complicated.
So-called industrial civilisation which was supposed to have made us all content and should have made us all clever and good and even aesthetes ... and then so-called

post-industrial civilisation and all the other post this and post-that industrial civilisations – whether by destiny or by choice or by destined choice I don't know – started to define themselves as ever more introvert and closed "cultures", increasingly organized around themselves; as "cultures" steadily more cryptic and isolated, farther and farther away, deafer and deafer to the frailty of human existence ... and the frailty of existence certainly was not erased. On the contrary, it might have unexpectedly worsened.
The languages, logic and codes that belong to new "cultures" are more or less hermetic; they have become by now mannered idioms, streams of logic and codes that emit no light.

During the Sixties and Seventies, entire young and not-so-young generations got scared when they sensed what was going on. They escaped in various ways: some in order to hide, some to avoid being around, some not to be involved. Some, who were really afraid, went into the woods and some tried to find time to understand what was behind everything that seemed so exaggeratedly chrome-plated ...
Some, who were poets, wrote poetry and some wrote songs; some printed books and booklets, some took photographs, and some who were destined to do drawings, did special drawings ...
Some of those people had an irresistible urge to see or even only to look for that modicum of "archaic, bare necessity" which might still be regained beyond the great lie announced by industrial culture, beyond the big, unfulfilled, promise of general happiness; beyond the ever-planned and by then unbearably boring mannerism which Institutions pursued and continue to pursue ... there were a few attempts to find alternative ways out.
Perhaps it was this constant effort that led some people in the profession to the trials and errors, to the disasters, hopes and ideas that later went – for example – by the name of Memphis ...

The first real glass things I designed for Memphis and produced with my friend Gigi Toso, were vases of more or less normal shapes, already seen and foreseen. I had altered those ancient forms with surface variations, with more or less unexpected or disconnected external additions. The attempt was to get away from set codes. Perhaps only the colour combinations were unusual: they certainly played an important part, by accelerating the "sensorial" perception of the object rather than echoing other possible withered metaphors or symbologies ...

It took a good deal of work and time to realise how much "erotic" potential could be expressed through glass, to understand just how far working with glass demands the attention of all the senses: a very special attention to thickness, distances, weights, colours, transparencies, overlapping transparencies and mixtures of transparencies; and then also to understand to what extent glass creates a special awareness of its fragility: and I'm talking about what glass itself asks for, which is to be treated with slow, precious gestures. In any case, even those gestures start from a possible sensorial rituality.
With all this on my mind, I grew agitated when I started designing the second series (made for Memphis), again with the help of Gigi Toso. A good-natured and patient man, he was particularly patient when I told him the glass pieces I had designed would need glue to hold them together.
At Murano as far as I know, the idea of using glue was nothing short of scandalous and I think that for the true, classic masters of the art it still is. Nevertheless, for my glass objects, glue was used to hold pieces together.
I also thought this idea of making pieces and then putting them on top of each other and attaching them to each other, had come to me because I am fated to think as an architect, because as soon as I was born my father (an architect) put a pencil in my hand. As if to say I was bound to become an architect and that's more or less the way it went.

Since Memphis, since I designed that second range of glass objects, I have always thought of glass made of pieces put together either with glue, or jointed or fitted into a support, like the latest ones designed for my friends Barovier and Bischofberger.
This idea of designing glass with pieces put together in one way or another – pieces of different coloured glass, different thicknesses, opacity and transparencies, of different sizes, shapes and origins – allowed me a great freedom of design. Most of all, it gave me an infinite catalogue of real, sensorial pleasures. It threw me into the open arms of glass as "erotic material", enabling me to recount long sensorial adventures. It became possible to mix colours in the least expected combinations, to produce new and unlikely "electric" states by matching glass with wood, marble and iron. I could imagine unpredictable balances of structures, and walk within the subtle realm of breathing and of rhythm ...
In any case, all those trials always concerned exercises, movements, juxtapositions, collages and acrobatics, performed with legible figures as a more or less abstract sensorial whole. For a long time I stayed within the field of neoplasticist manoeuvres

– if I might so call those exercises in colours, forms, figures and rhythms that live on nothing but themselves and never encroach on memories or nostalgia, symbols or enigmas... on literature.

## IV

Then, getting older maybe, perhaps through one of those mysterious bits of information that reach us silently from the movements of history, I began to recognize that by now I certainly can't imagine myself as an abstract being ... I mean a being that tries to live by abstractions.
As the years go by I feel more and more as if I were built out of a very complicated chemical mixture in continuous agitation: a chemistry of memories, nostalgia, fear and vital energies, of hopes and aggressiveness, sacrifices, names that come and go, exhaustive answers that fade away ... to pose other questions.
Sometimes I think that if I design something in glass – and not only in glass – I may also try to leave some trace, some sign of this new perception that gives me perhaps a broader, certainly more complex, definitely less conceited idea of existence.
Perhaps now I can leave a few signs, at least a few signs of affection, for all those ghosts drifting in from the past and from the future to crowd my time ....

That's what I have tried to do in the latest glass objects, the ones done with Venini, for Bruno Bischofberger and in those done with Cenedese, for Marino and Marina Barovier.

**ETTORE SOTTSASS**
**April 6th, 1998**

(Translated from Italian by Rodney Stringer)

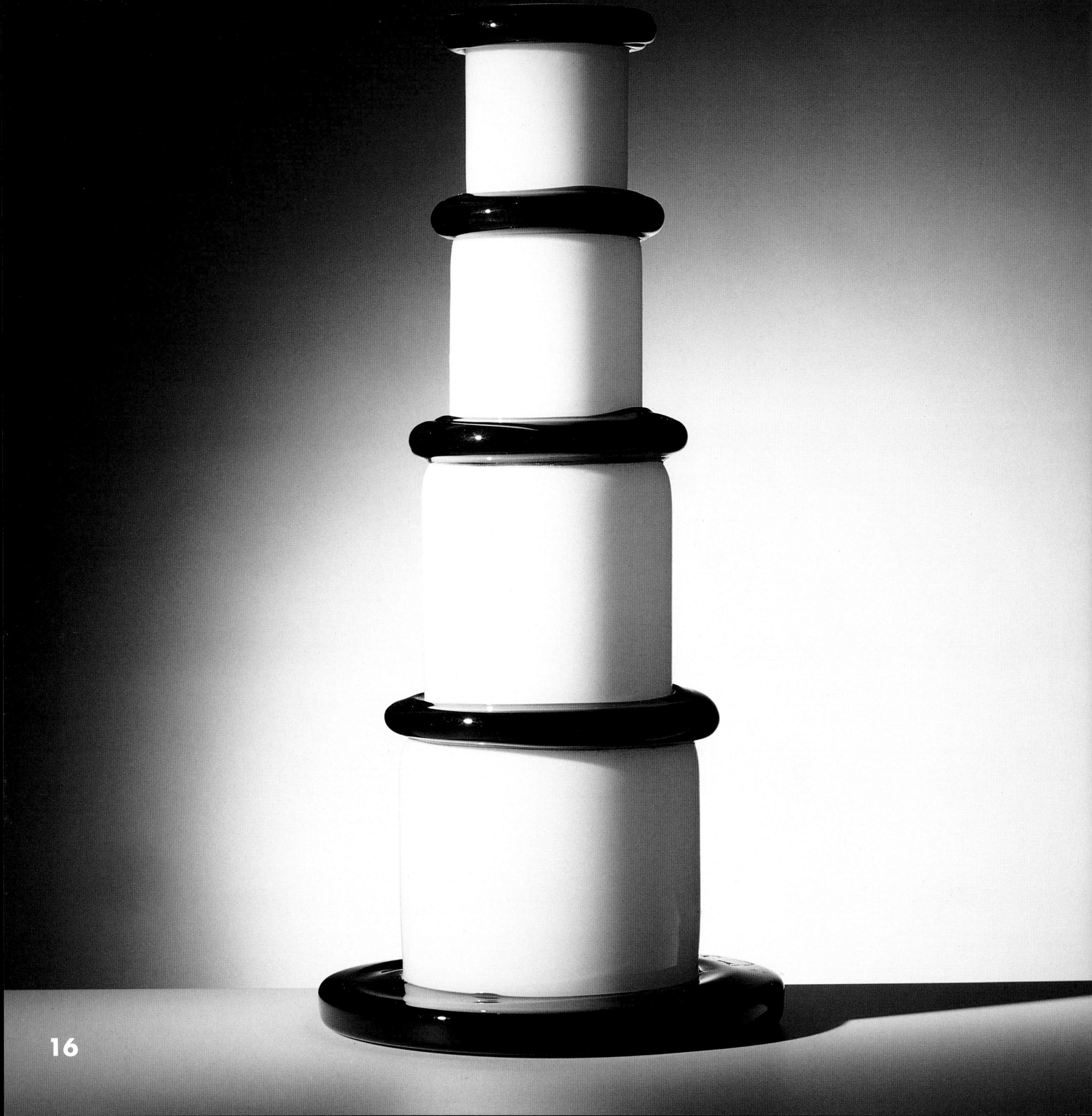

19.3.83
SOTTSASS

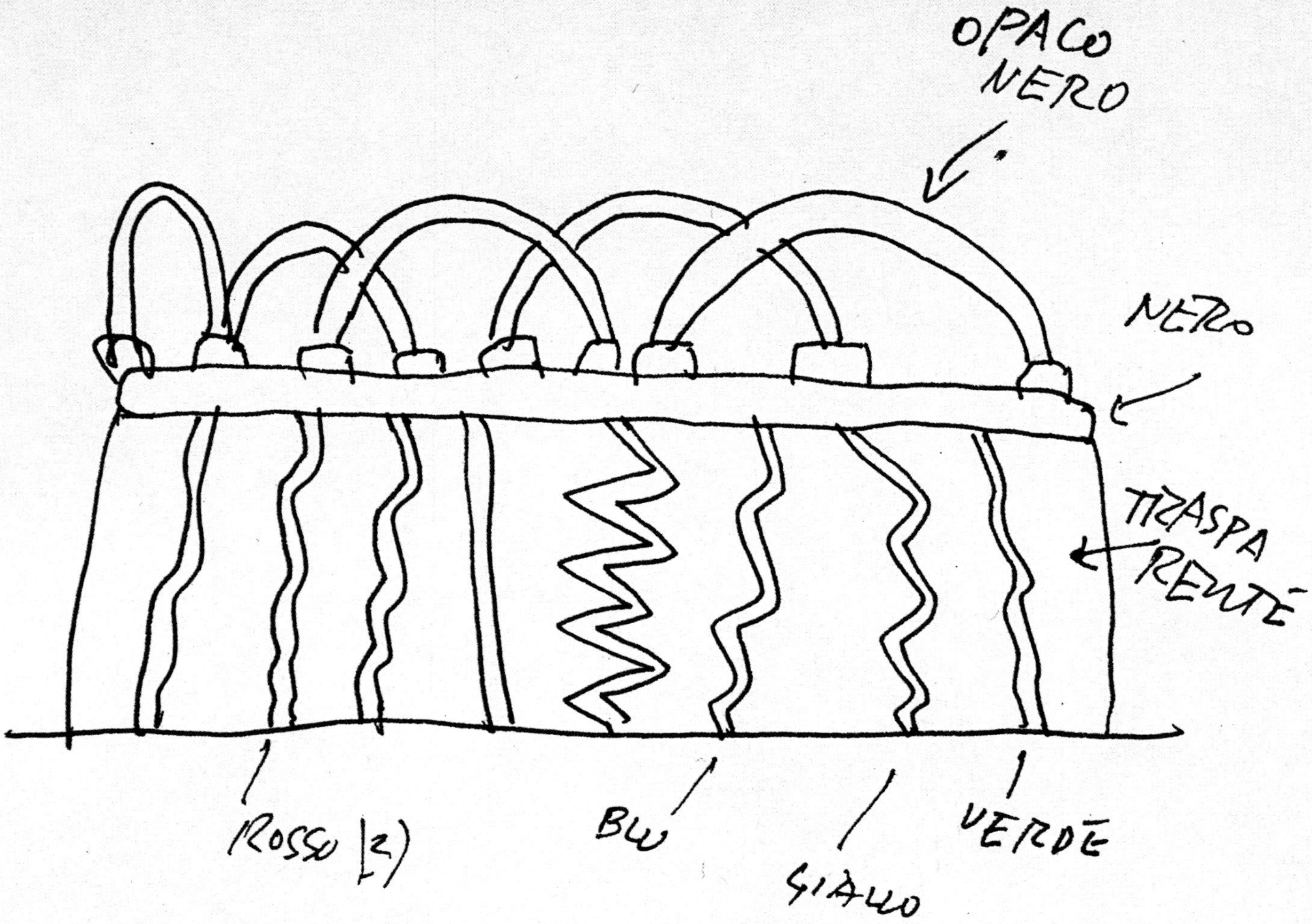
OPACO
NERO
NERO
TRASPA
RENTE
ROSSO (2)
BLU
GIALLO
VERDE

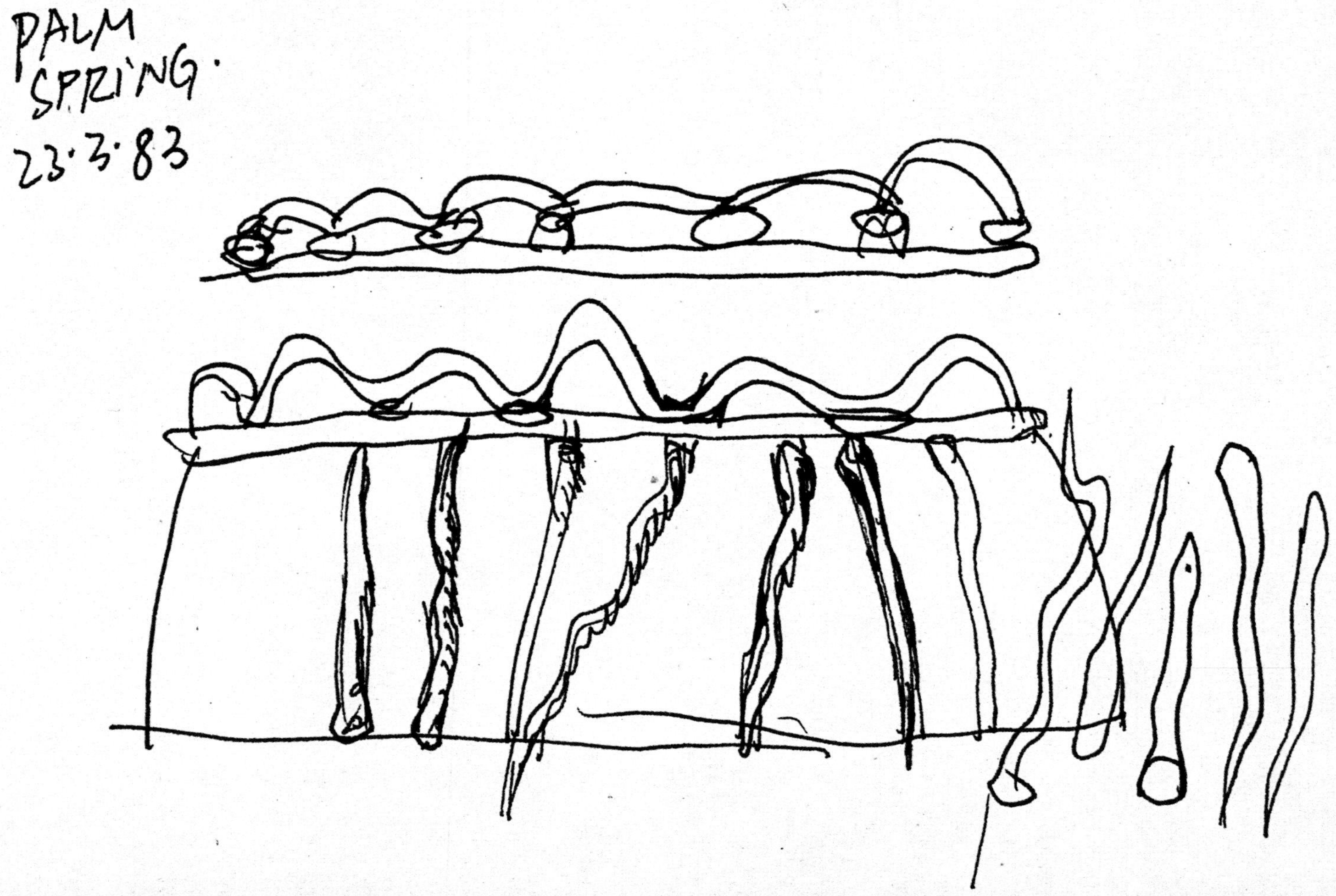
PALM
SPRING.
23.3.83

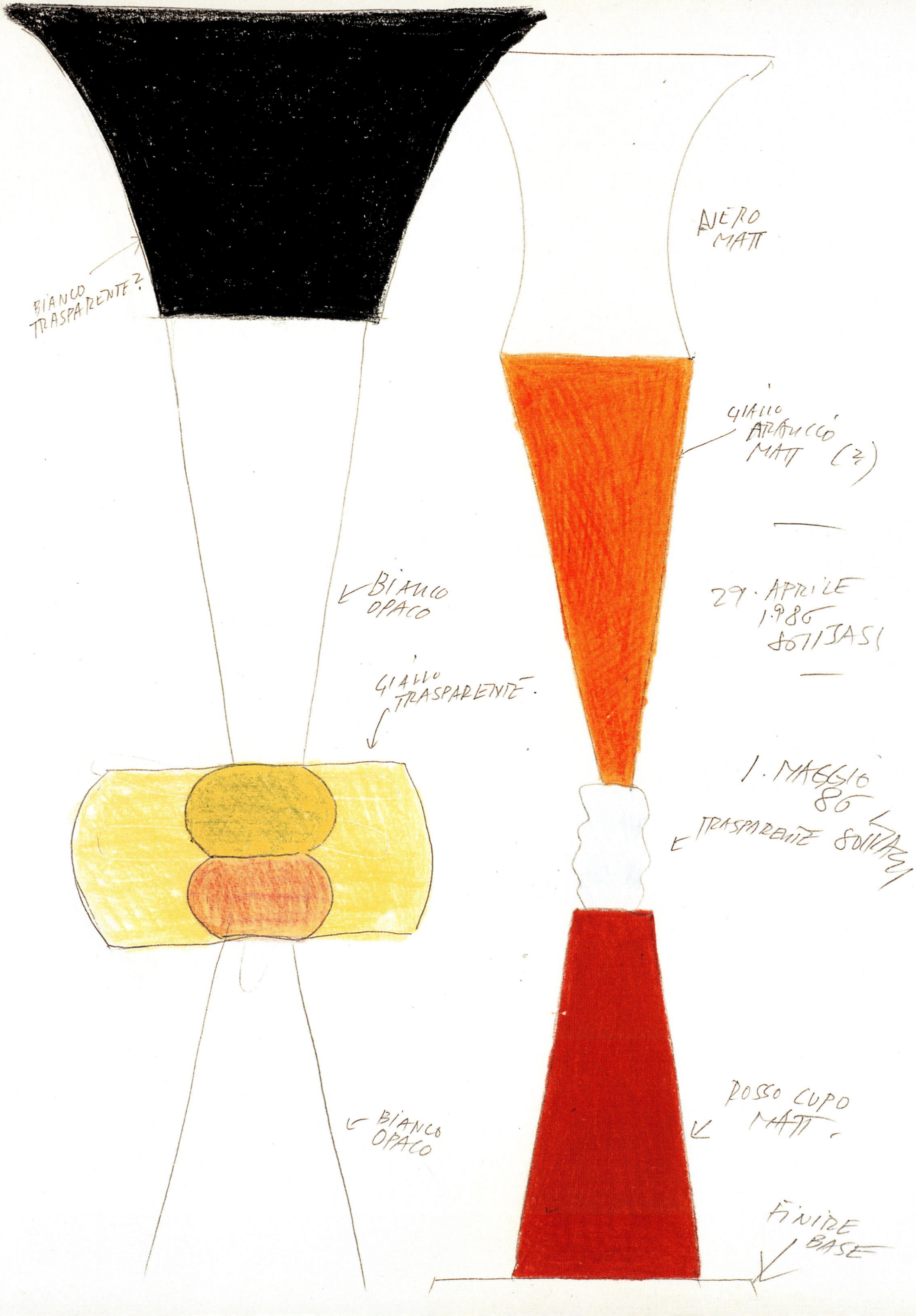
BIANCO TRASPARENTE?
NERO MATT
BIANCO OPACO
GIALLO TRASPARENTE.
29. APRILE 1986 SOTTSASS
1. MAGGIO 86
TRASPARENTE
ROSSO CUPO MATT.
BIANCO OPACO
FINIRE BASE

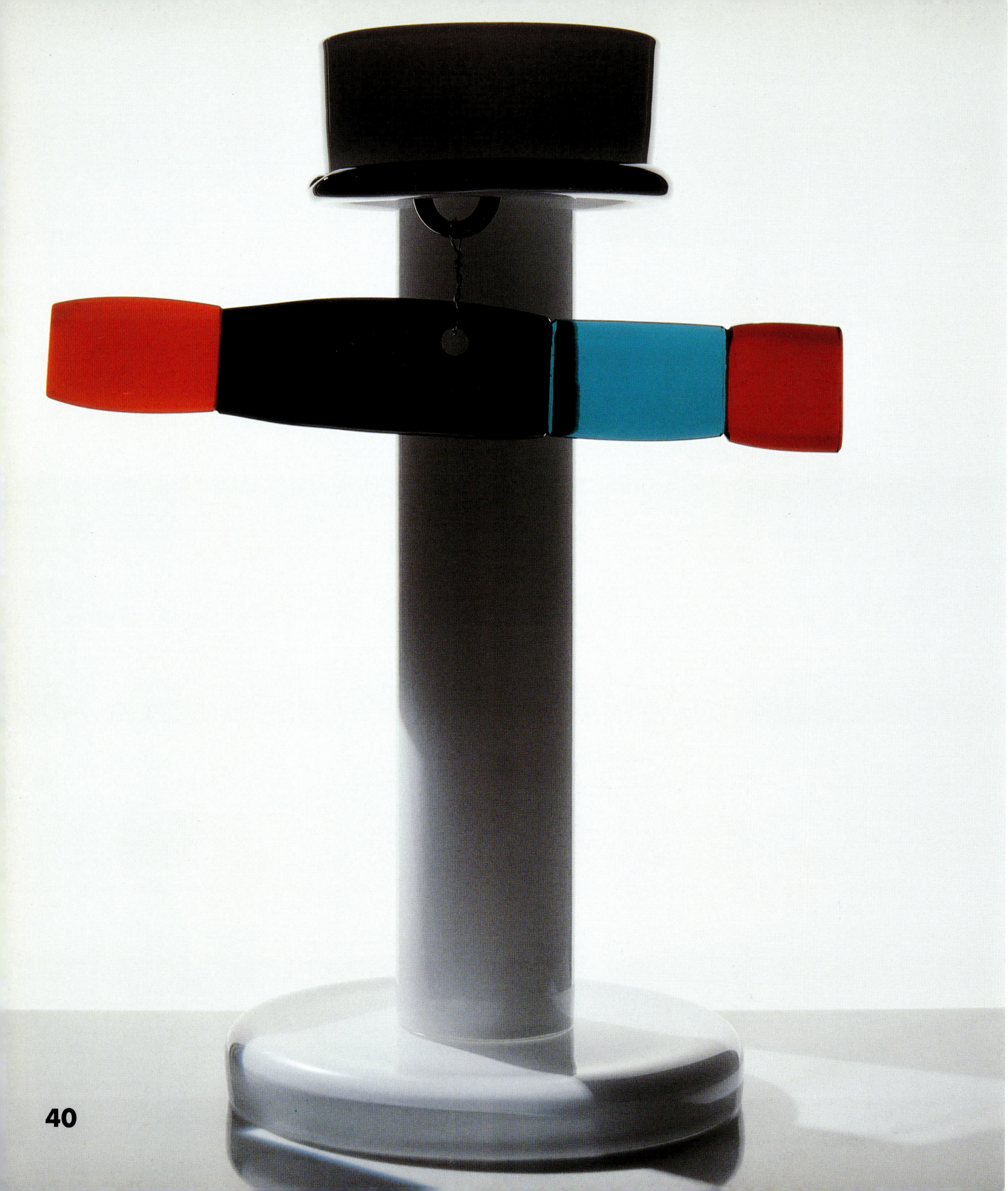

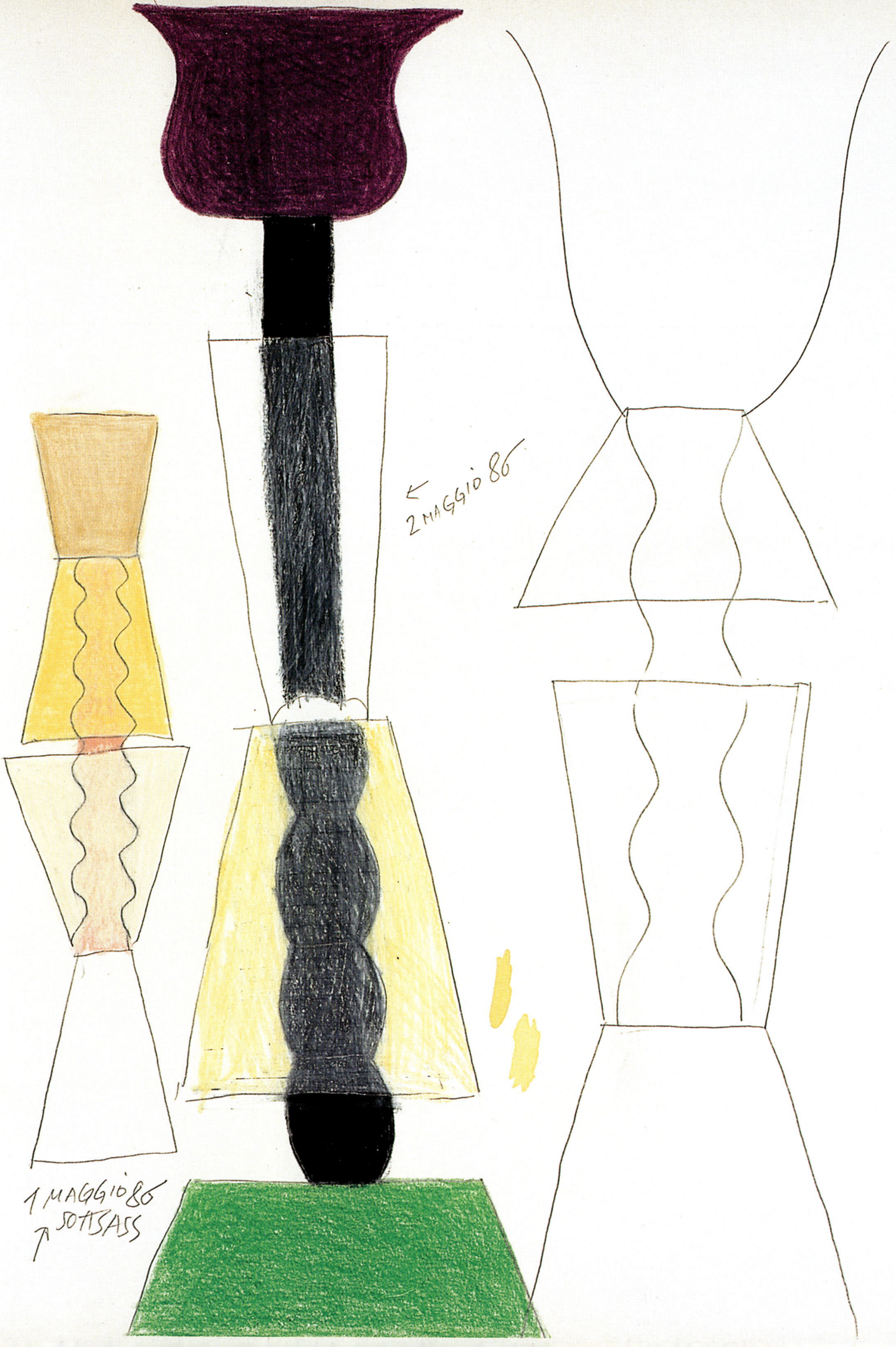
← 2 MAGGIO 86
1 MAGGIO 86
SOTTSASS

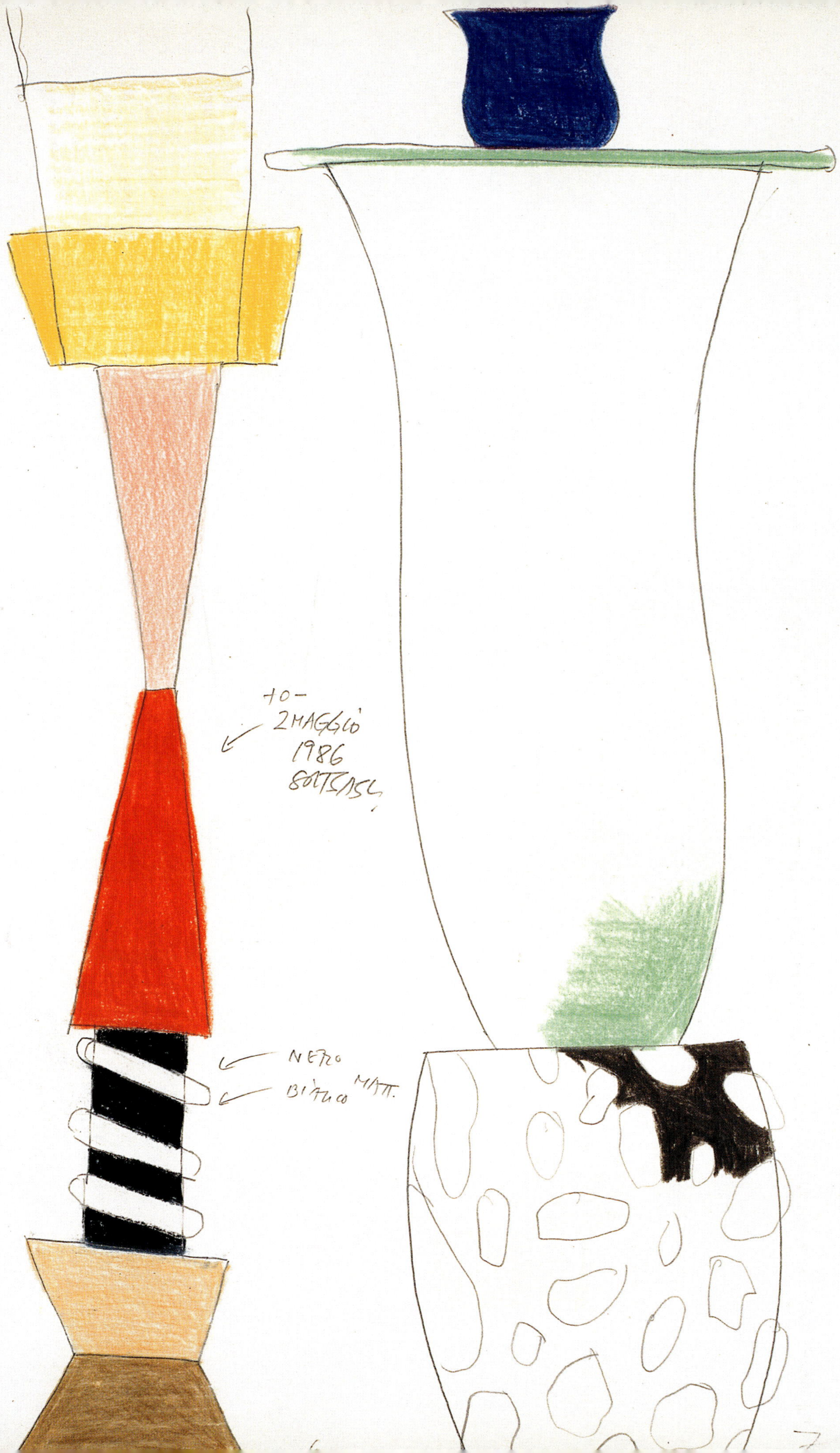
2 MAGGIO
1986
NERO
BIANCO
MATT.

MILANO
1 MAGGIO 86
SOTTSASS
3
4

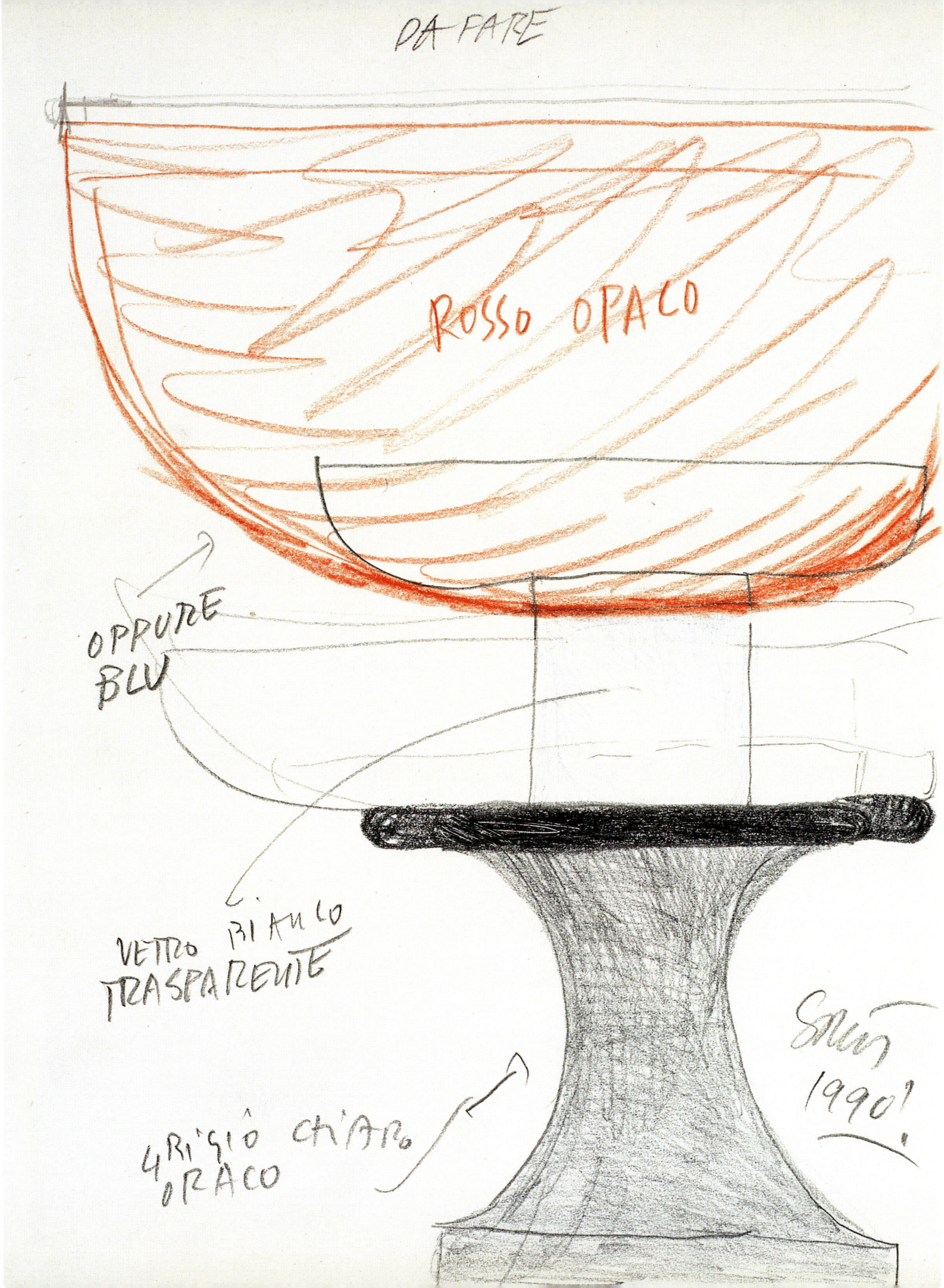
DA FARE
ROSSO OPACO
OPPURE
BLU
VETRO BIANCO
TRASPARENTE
GRIGIO CHIARO
OPACO
1990!

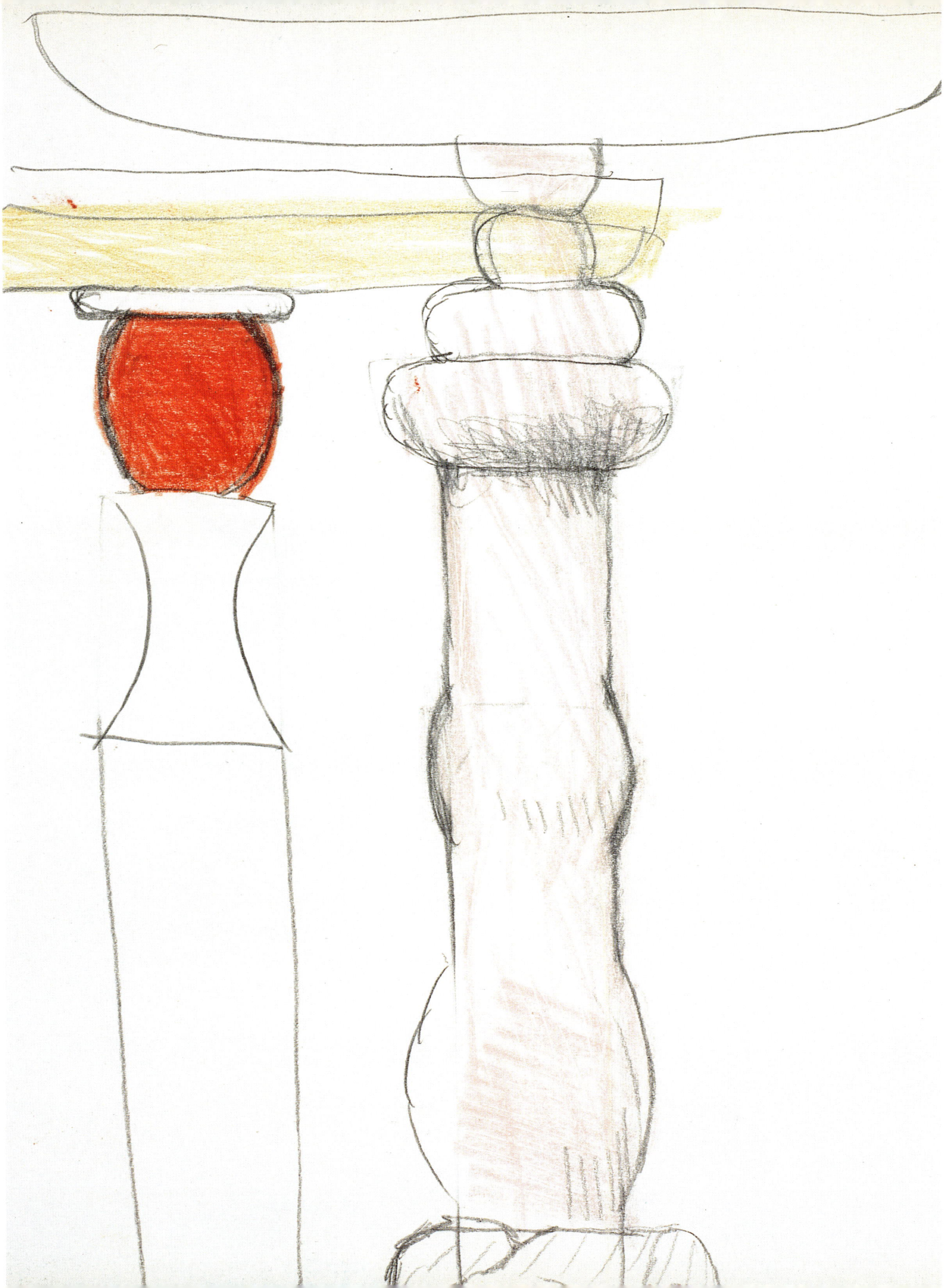

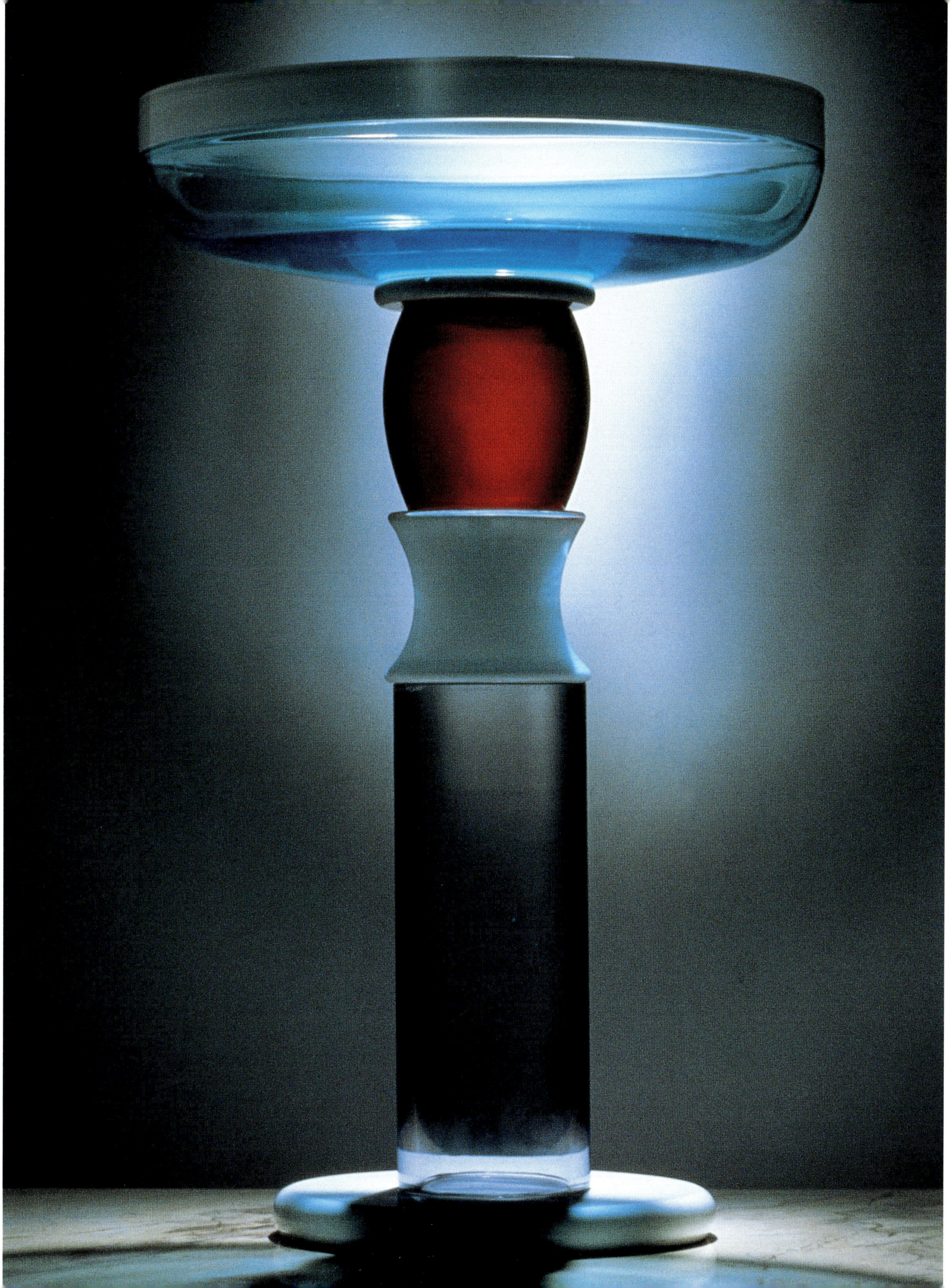

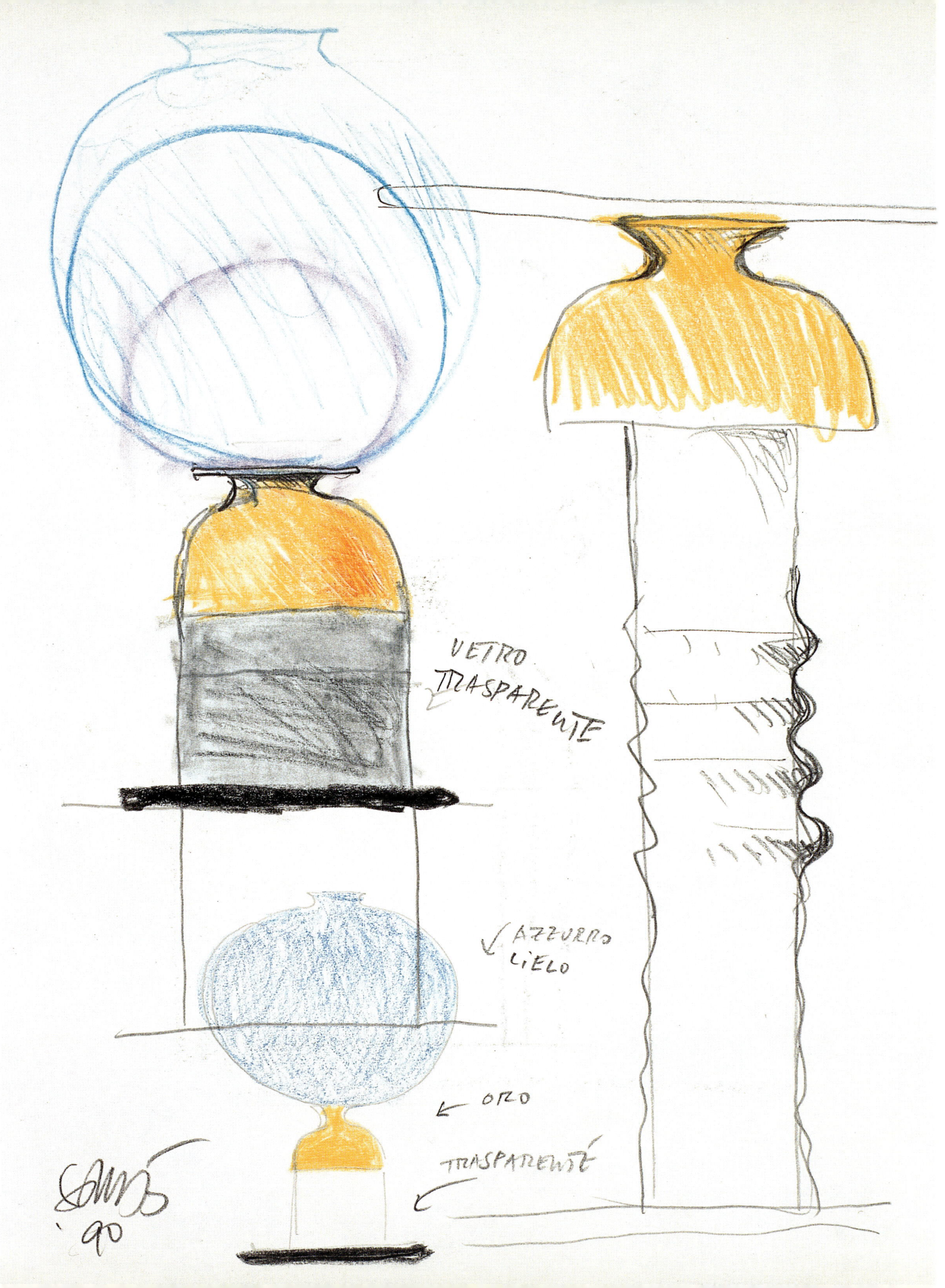
VETRO TRASPARENTE
AZZURRO CIELO
ORO
TRASPARENTE
'90

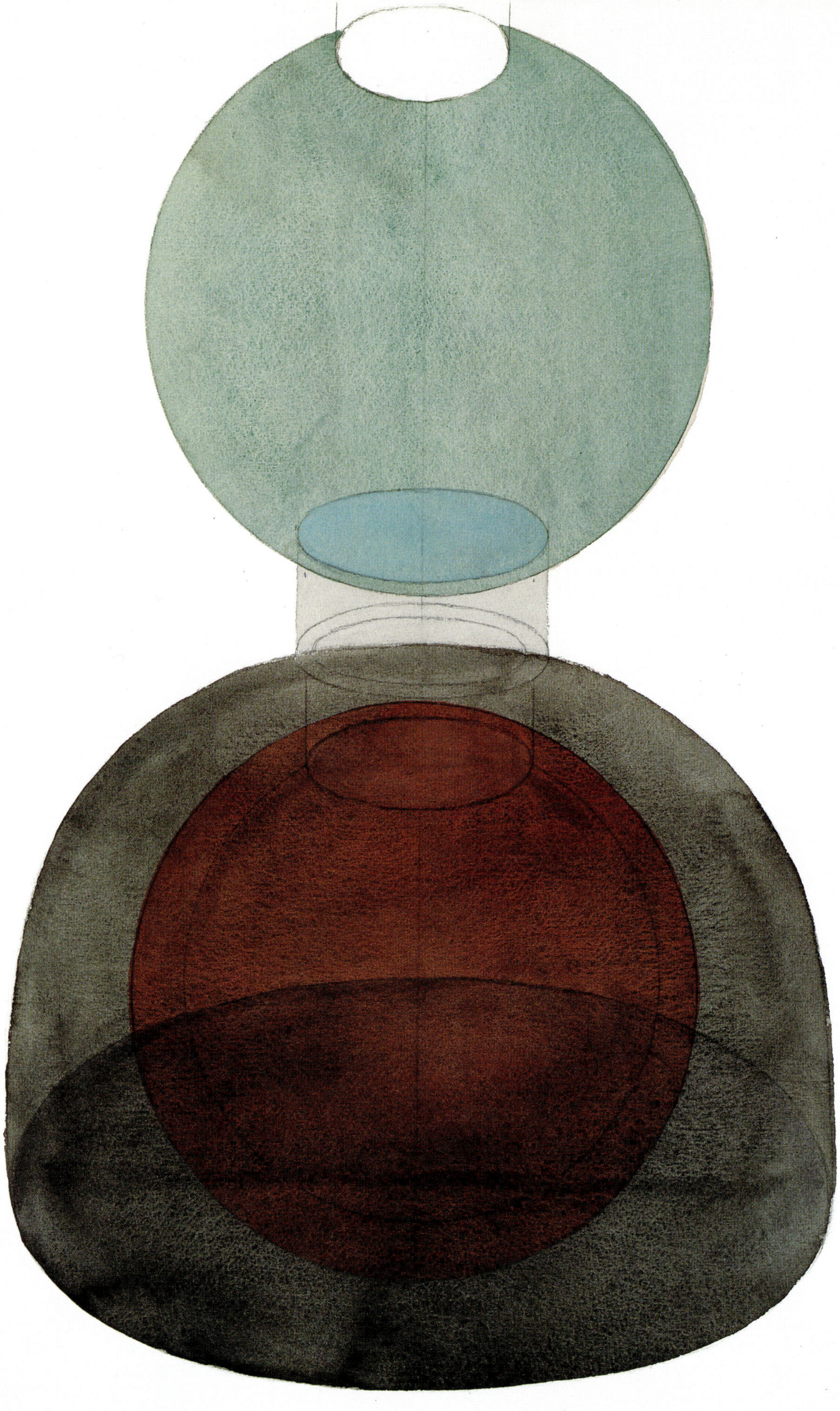

NERO
STOFFA
DA FARÉ
FATTO
STUPA
RUGGINE
BLACK HOLE

NAOMI CAMPBELL
BLU ?
TURCHESE
VERDE SCURO
L'ALBERO
BLU SCURO FORTE
MARRONE GRIGIO O VERDE
NERI
5 BETILI

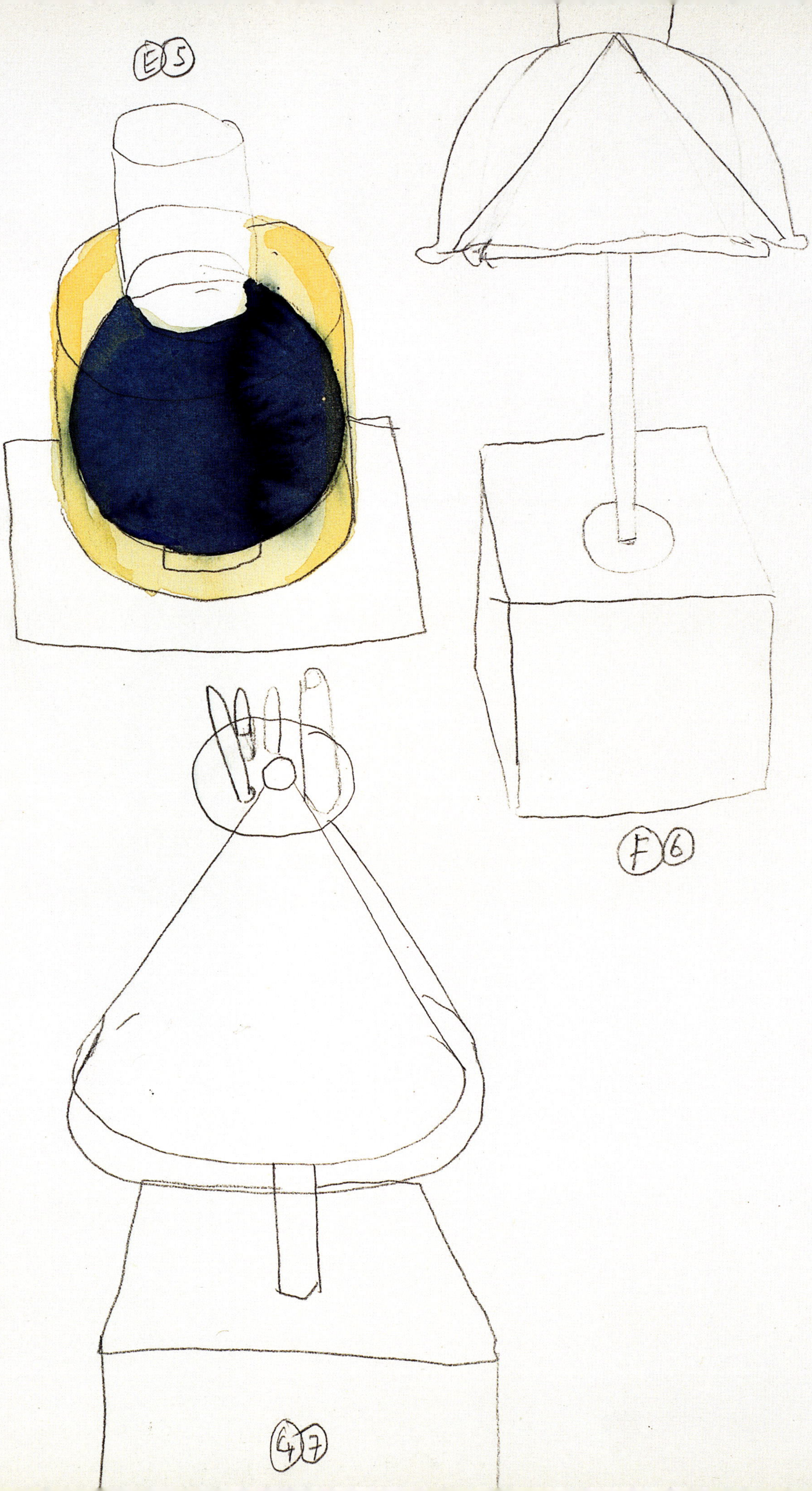
E 5
F 6
G 7

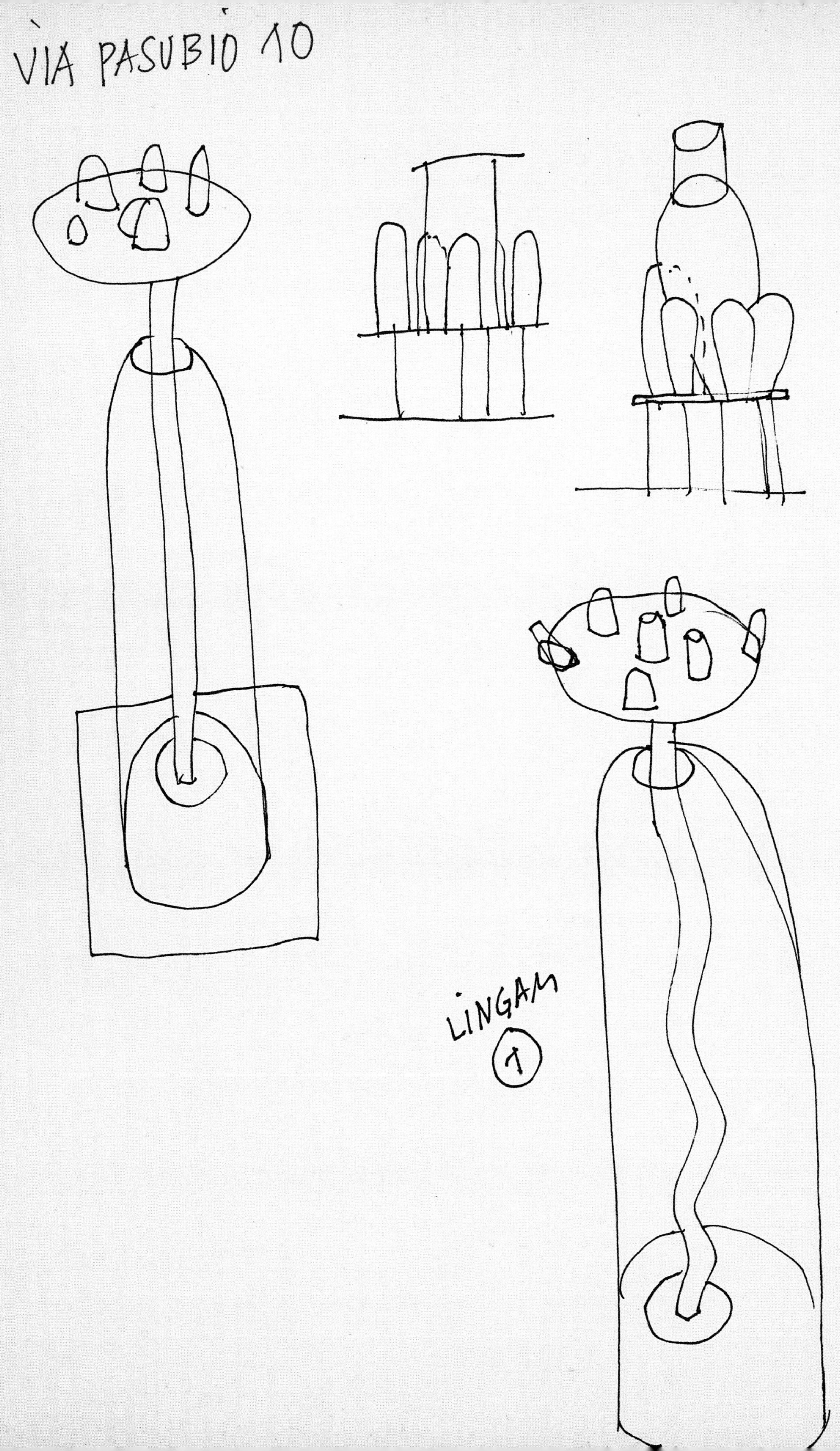
VÌA PASUBIO 10
LINGAM
1

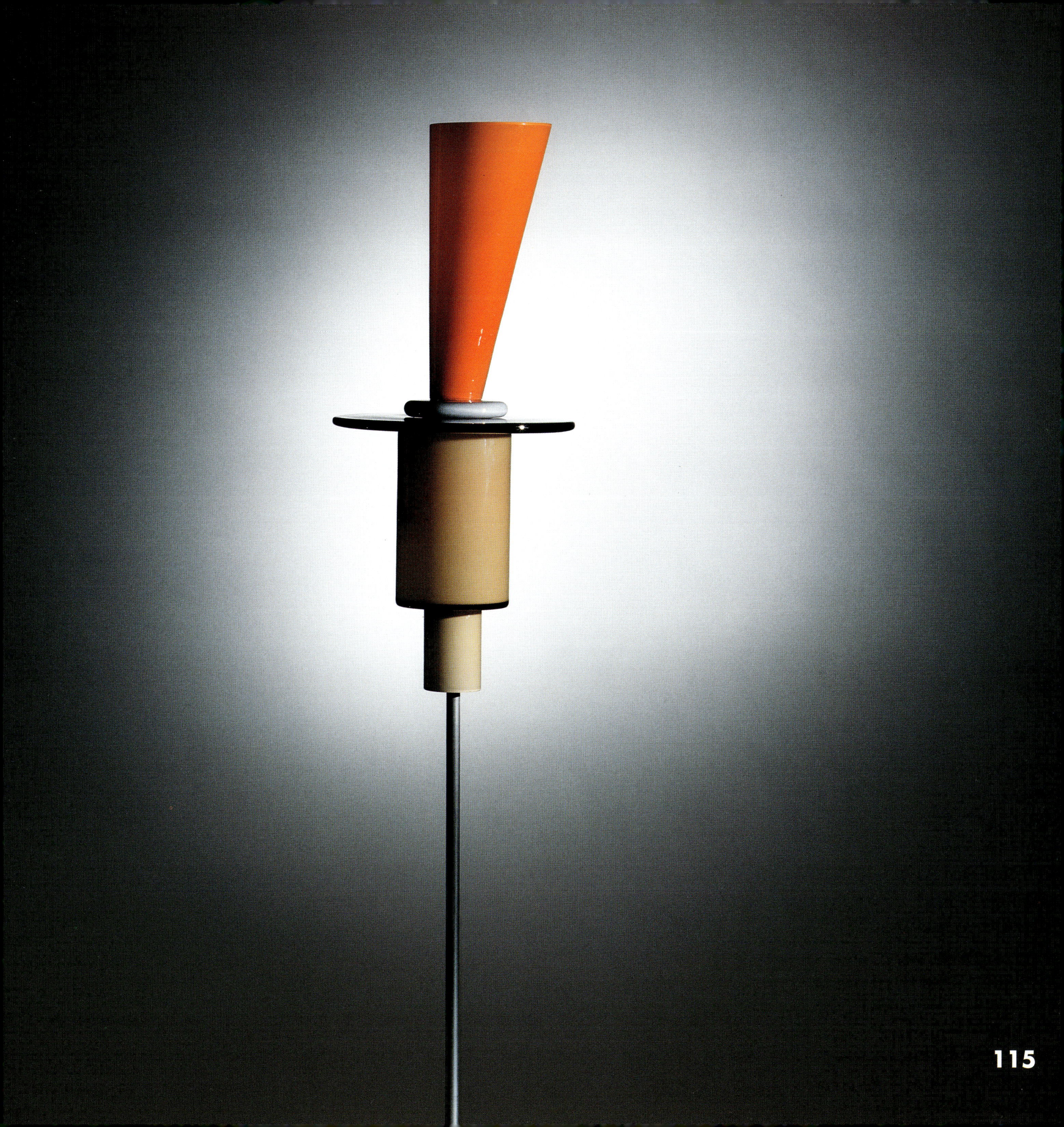

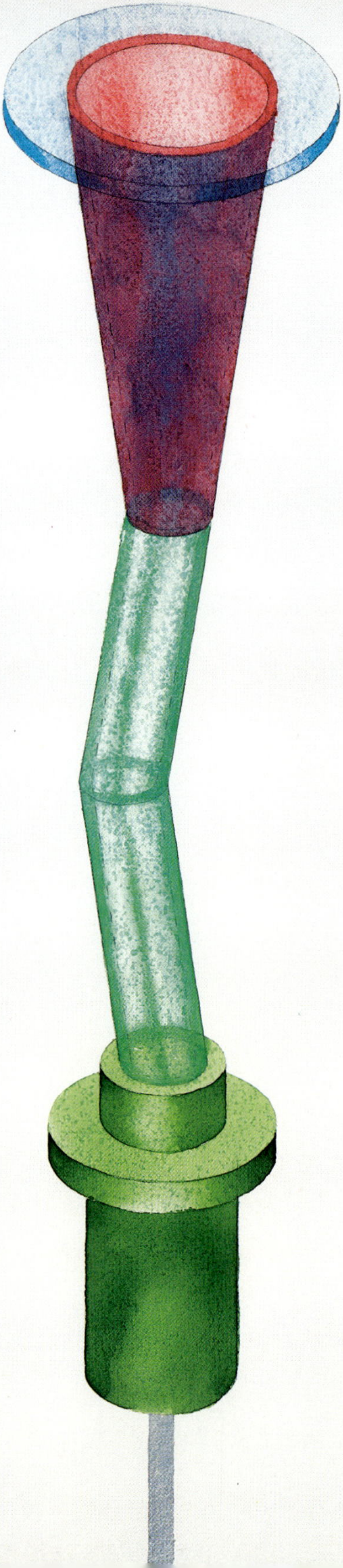

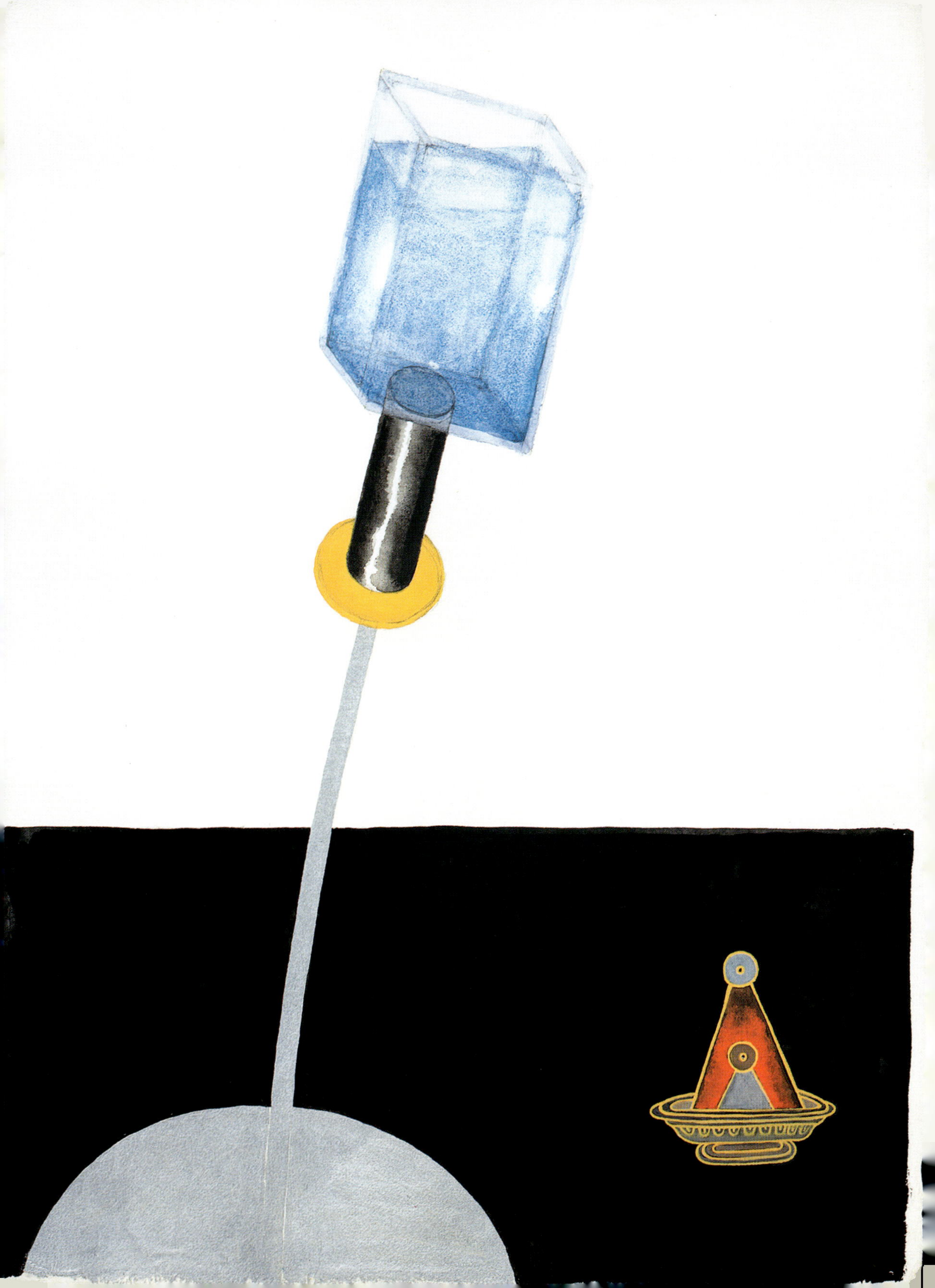

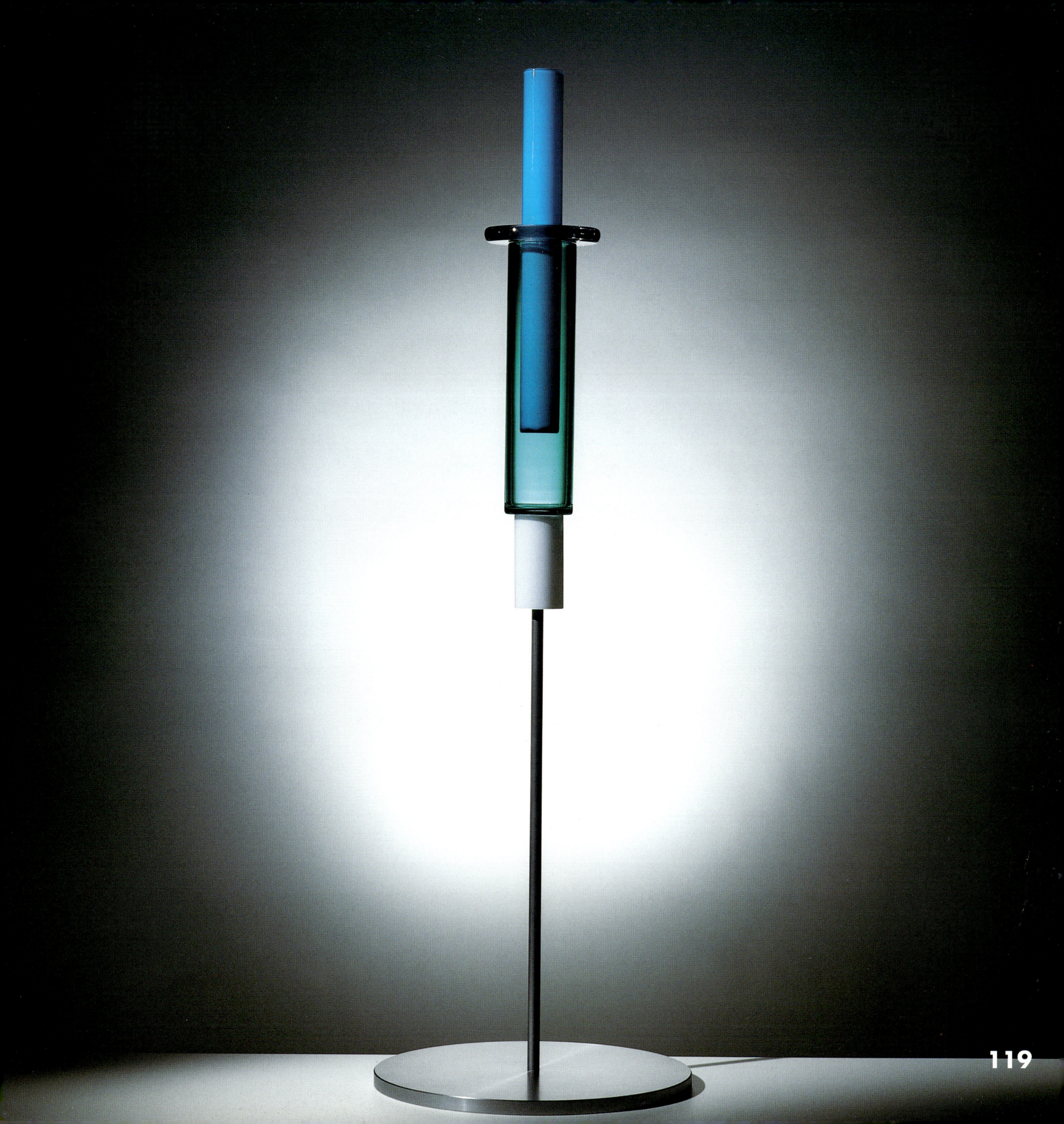

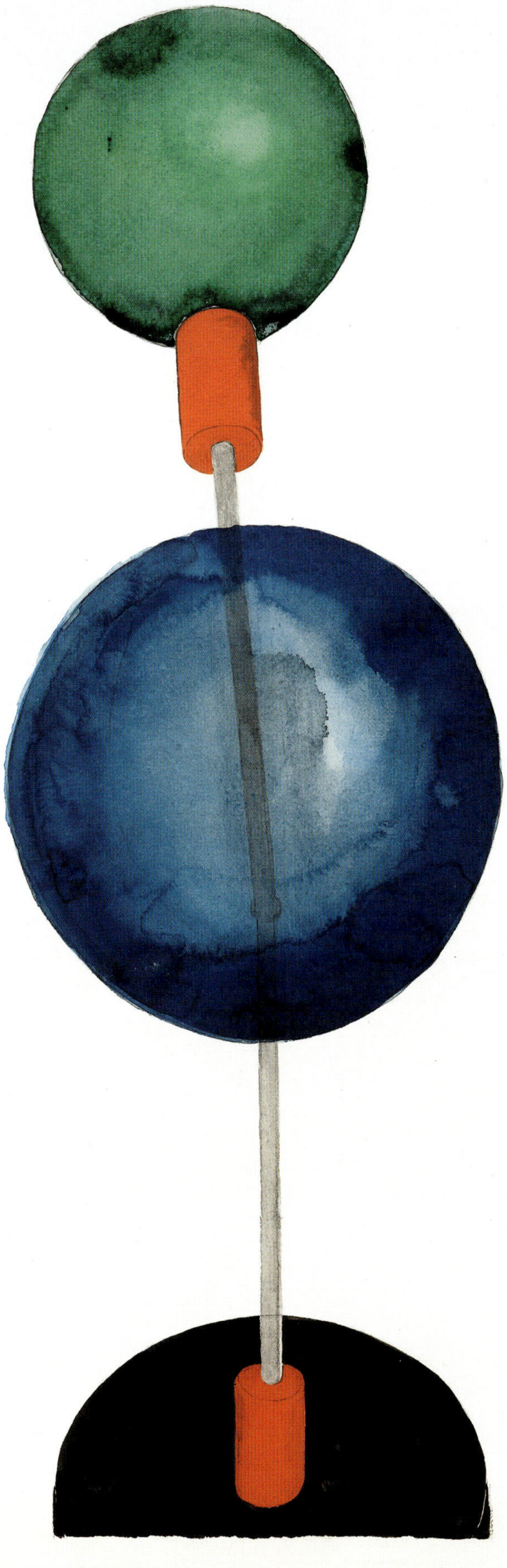

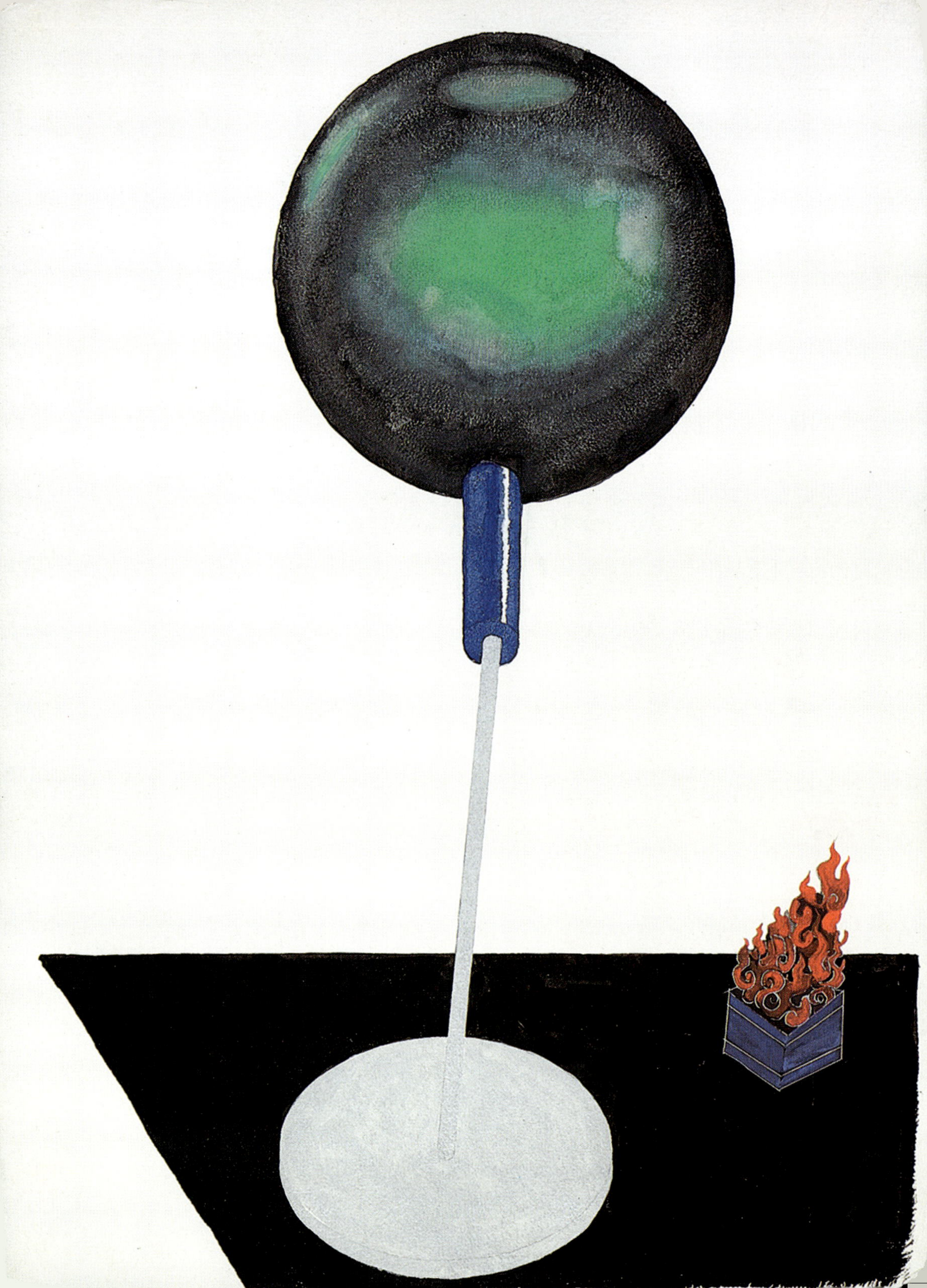

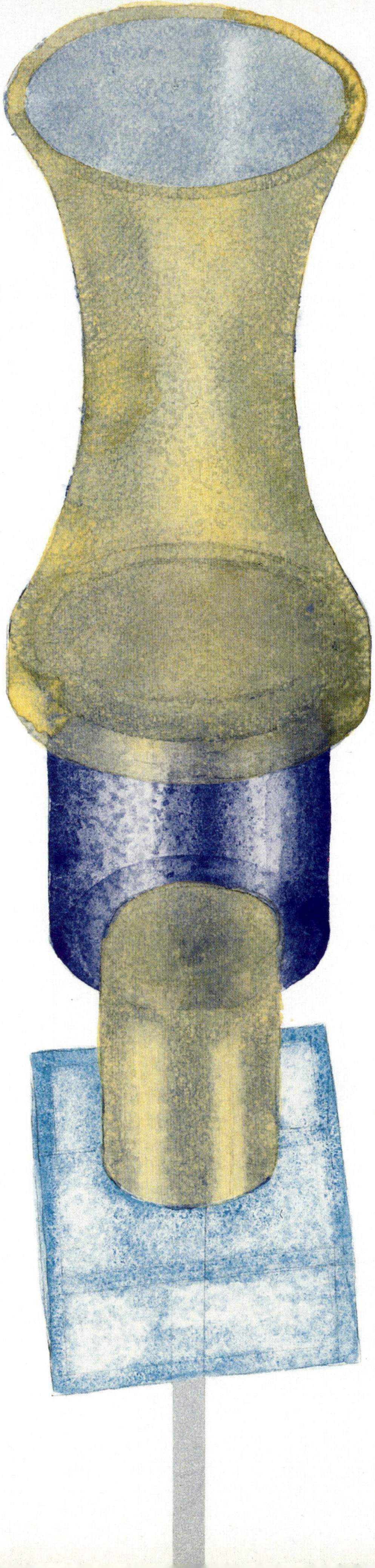

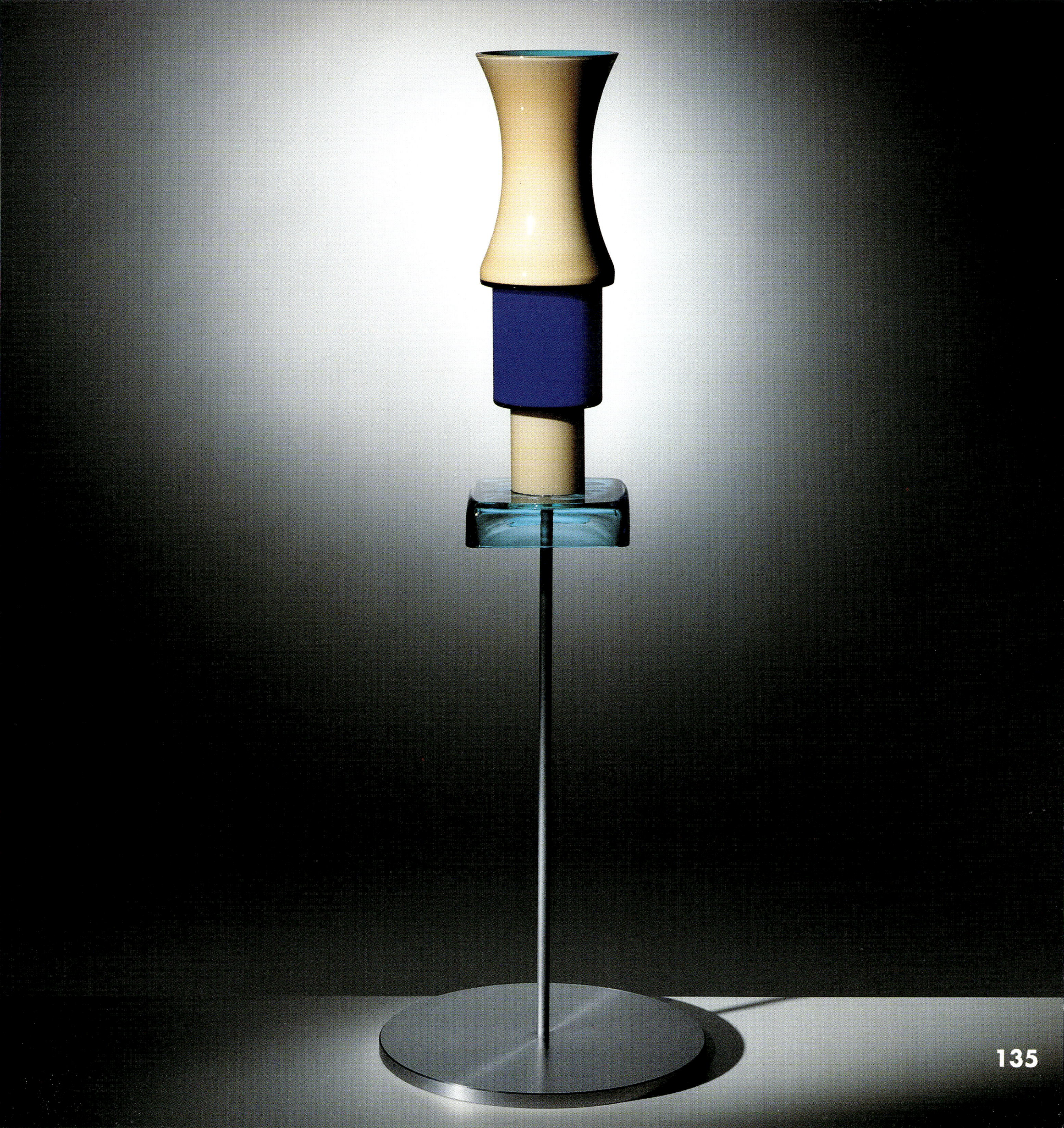

4
POCO TRASPARENTE
5
PIETRA SERENA
2
1

114.–